A City of Synonyms

Synonyms are words that have nearly the same meaning.

big   large

Read the sentences. Write a **synonym** from the box to replace each underlined word.

dashed	**desired**	**drowsy**	**enjoyable**	**freezing**
greatest	**journeyed**	**observed**	**overwhelmed**	**thrilled**	**whole**

1. New York is a <u>fun</u> place to visit. _____

2. During the winter months, the city can be <u>cold</u>! _____

3. I <u>watched</u> people ice skate in Rockefeller Plaza. _____

4. My family <u>rode</u> through Central Park in a carriage. _____

5. My dad got <u>sleepy</u> on the trip. _____

6. Mom and I <u>ran</u> from store to store on 5th Avenue. _____

7. I was <u>excited</u> to get the exact tee shirt I <u>wanted</u> as a souvenir.

    _____   _____

8. It was the <u>best</u> vacation ever. _____

9. When I got home, I rested for an <u>entire</u> day. _____

10. My friends were <u>overcome</u> with joy to see me. _____

Challenge yourself!
Use a separate sheet of paper to create a list of your own synonyms.

Amazing Antonyms

Antonyms are words that have opposite meanings.

still   **moving**

Write an **antonym** for the underlined word to complete each sentence.
Use a dictionary if you need help.

1. Karen was not <u>late</u> for school because the bus came _____.

2. She <u>started</u> her day with a good breakfast and _____ it with a healthy dinner.

3. First, she _____ her books, but then she <u>found</u> them.

4. Karen was <u>happy</u> to arrive at school, but _____ because she forgot her lunch.

5. At school, she noticed her shirt was <u>clean</u>, but her pants were _____.

6. She <u>disliked</u> her history class but _____ her math class.

7. Her history teacher gave <u>vague</u> directions, and her math teacher's directions were _____.

8. After school, Karen had an <u>immense</u> amount of homework and _____ play time.

9. She <u>made</u> a science project and hoped her little brother wouldn't _____ it.

10. It was a long <u>day</u>, and Karen couldn't wait to get a good _____'s rest.

11. Karen likes to go to bed <u>early</u> and wake up _____.

12. Most of the time, Karen is <u>healthy</u> but now and then she gets _____.

13. Her room is very <u>colorful</u>, while her sister's is very _____.

Picture Perfect Homophones

Homophones are words that sound alike but have different spellings and meanings.

Read each sentence. Circle the **homophone** that correctly completes it.

1. Last (weak, week) we went to the movies.

2. When I see sad movies like that one, I (ball, bawl).

3. We (ate, eight) so much popcorn my stomach was sick for a week.

4. An (our, hour) after the movies my family and I went out to dinner.

5. I was sad because my baseball cap (blew, blue) off my head.

6. I didn't know (wear, where) it landed, so I never found it.

7. My (ant, aunt) wants to take me to see a comedy movie.

8. I (here, hear) the best movies are coming out this summer!

9. When I get older, I would love to land a (role, roll) as an actor.

10. I (know, no) I would enjoy acting for a living.

11. My neighbors said (their, there) daughter had been in a commercial once.

12. She was scared during filming because the commercial's star was a (bare, bear)!

13. I'd love to be in a commercial with a (dear, deer) because it's my favorite animal.

14. (Its, It's) a great paying job when you are young.

Challenge yourself!
Write a post card to a relative about your plans for the summer. Be sure to include at least five homophones.

Batting Up With Compound Words

A **compound word** is formed by two or more single words

base + ball =

baseball

Match each word in column A with a word in column B to form a compound word. Then match each word in column C with a word in column D.

A	B		C	D
1. air	quake		7. grand	chair
2. pillow	shoe		8. brother	mother
3. sea	shell		9. boat	hood
4. earth	case		10. arm	ball
5. horse	plane		11. basket	lace
6. flash	light		12. shoe	house

Read the paragraphs below and underline the compound words.

Carter's favorite sport is baseball. He plays on a team every weekend in the spring and summer. He often daydreams about becoming a professional baseball player.

Carter's number one cheerleader is his mother. She comes to every game. Carter can often see her cheering from the dugout. If he gets butterflies in his stomach before he goes up to bat, looking at his mom helps him calm down. He knows that after the game, Mom will make his favorite meal, hotdogs and watermelon, which they will eat outside in the backyard.

Challenge yourself!
Draw a funny picture of a compound word.
For example, a hot dog could look like this.
Use a separate sheet of paper.

Understanding compound words

Common Contractions

A **contraction** is a shortened word made by joining two words. Some letters of one word are dropped and an apostrophe takes their place.

She **was not** home when I called her.

She **wasn't** home when I called her.

Library Rules

did not didn't

Write the contraction for the underlined words.

1. The library <u>is</u> <u>not</u> open on Sundays. _____

2. I <u>can</u> <u>not</u> wait until the summer library program begins. _____

3. I <u>have</u> <u>not</u> read all of my favorite books yet. _____

4. Joe says <u>he</u> <u>will</u> join the summer program. _____

5. Andy and Kim said they <u>would</u> <u>not</u> be able to join this year. _____

6. <u>They</u> <u>will</u> have to wait until the following summer. _____

Write the contraction for each set of words.

7. **should not** _____	**you have** _____
8. **he will** _____	**could not** _____
9. **I am** _____	**they will** _____
10. **is not** _____	**there will** _____
11. **was not** _____	**has not** _____
12. **do not** _____	**are not** _____
13. **will not** _____	**I will** _____
14. **they are** _____	**she will** _____
15. **he is** _____	**she is** _____

Challenge yourself!
You have formed a friendship club. Create a list of rules for your club on a separate sheet of paper. Include contractions in each rule.

Presenting Prefixes

A **prefix** is a word part added to the beginning of a base, or root, word at the beginning. The prefix changes the meaning of the base word.

Match each prefix with its meaning. Use a dictionary if you need help.

Prefix	Meaning
1. pre-	again, back
2. un-	before
3. re-	not
4. dis-	against
5. mis-	from, take away from
6. anti-	opposite of
7. de-	half
8. semi-	wrong

Use the prefixes and base words to create a new word for each definition.

Prefixes
pre- un- re- dis- mis- in-

Base Words
consider paid spelled pleasant appear separable

9. to make vanish   ___disappear___   to pay before _____

10. to not spell correctly _____   not enjoyable _____

11. to consider again _____   together _____

Read the paragraphs and circle the words with prefixes.

   A magician has an unbelievable job! I'd like to be a magician. I don't think I would feel uncomfortable in front of an audience. I would make sure to be prepared to put on a good show—one that would earn rave reviews!

   My friends enjoy watching me perform magic tricks. If I became a famous magician I would give my friends a preview of my act the night before. I wonder if I could learn how to disappear before their eyes!

The Power of the Suffix

A **suffix** is a word part added to the end of a base, or root word. A suffix can change the meaning of the word.

Match each suffix with its meaning. Use a dictionary if you need help.

Suffix	Meaning
1. -able	without
2. -ful	worthy of or able to
3. -less	having, being that
4. -y	full of, having those qualities
5. -ly	in a certain way
6. -ment	superlative
7. -er	one who believes or does something
8. -est	result of
9. -ness	doer
10. -ist	state of being

Use the suffixes and base words to create a new word for each definition.

Base Words
like   orgranize   move   fame   small   hope

Suffixes
-ment -er -est -ness -ful -ous

11. one who organizes. _____organizer_____

extremely small _____

12. result of moving _____

to have fame _____

13. when something resembles _____

full of hope _____

Read the paragraph and circle the words with suffixes.

My friend Sam is an accomplished violinist. He plays his music beautifully. His recitals are enjoyable and entertaining for everyone. Sam's brother Joe is a harpist. Joe began playing the harp professionally after years of training. Sam hopes to be just as successful as Joe one day.

So Many Kinds of Sentences

A **complete sentence** tells a complete thought, or idea.
There are four grammatical types of sentences.

Kinds of Sentences	Examples	Punctuation
Declarative (Statement)	It is Lacey's birthday.	.
Interrogative (Question)	When is Lacey's birthday?	?
Imperative (Command)	Show me the party invitation.	.
Exclamatory (Exclamation)	I'm so excited for the party!	!

Identify each sentence below as declarative, interrogative, imperative, or exclamatory.

1. It's time for the wheat harvest! _____

2. How do farmers know when the wheat is ripe? _____

3. Too much rain can delay the harvest. _____

4. We must harvest the wheat tomorrow! _____

5. Please get the field equipment ready. _____

6. How long does it take to harvest the wheat? _____

Rewrite each sentence to form the sentence type named in the parentheses.

7. The fields of wheat look like oceans of gold. (exclamatory)

_____

8. What different kinds of large equipment are used to harvest the wheat? (declarative)

_____

9. My father has been harvesting wheat since he was a small child. (interrogative)

_____

10. Farmers like to finish the harvest before bad weather arrives. (imperative)

_____

Who? Did What?

The **subject** of the sentence tells whom or what the sentence is about.
The **predicate** tells what the subject does or is.

Circle the subject and underline the predicate in each sentence.

1. Shelby enjoys working at the family pet store.

2. She has many chores and duties to fulfill.

3. The small puppies are held on a daily basis.

4. The kittens like to have all the attention.

5. Shelby likes to help out in any way.

6. This young girl likes to earn her allowance.

A **compound subject** has more than one subject that shares the predicate.
A **compound predicate** has two or more actions or verbs performed by the subject.

Read each sentence. Circle **CS** if it has a compound subject or **CP** if it has a
compound predicate. If it has both, circle both.

7. The pet store is run by the entire family.	**CS**	**CP**
8. Shelby's father owns and operates the store.	**CS**	**CP**
9. Her mother and father try to work everyday.	**CS**	**CP**
10. Sometimes grandma will help clean and move the cages.	**CS**	**CP**
11. Uncle Dale and Aunt Kathy like to help out, too.	**CS**	**CP**
12. Uncle Dale has built and painted many of the shelves.	**CS**	**CP**
13. Polly and Clair have baked and decorated a cake.	**CS**	**CP**
14. The family enjoys playing and caring for the animals.	**CS**	**CP**

So Many Thoughts

A complete simple sentence tells one complete thought.
A compound sentence contains two or more complete simple sentences or thoughts, often joined by a conjunction such as **and**, **but**, or **or**.

I enjoy snow skiing. I hope I don't break my leg.

Complete simple sentences: Snow skiing is fun.
You must be careful while you ski.

Compound sentence: Snow skiing is fun, but you must be careful while you ski.

Read each sentence. Write **S** if it is simple or **C** if it is compound.

1. My family and I go skiing each winter in Colorado. _____
2. My brother likes to snowboard, but dad likes to use two skis. _____
3. My sister Jean will try skiing again this time. _____
4. She wants to ride the lift up on her own this year. _____
5. Last year she tried to ride the lift, but she was too frightened. _____
6. My mother had to help her off, and Jean was embarrassed. _____

Combine the two simple sentences to make a compound sentence using **and**, **but**, or **or**.

7. My family shopped for skiing supplies. We all didn't find what we needed.

_____

_____

8. My brother found the gloves he liked. He found the suit he wanted.

_____

_____

9. The suit was bright red. It had racing stripes.

_____

_____

10. My brother thought he might buy it. He could use his old suit another year.

_____

_____

Understanding simple and compound sentences

No Run-Ons Allowed!

Run-On Sentences

A **run-on sentence** contains two or more sentences that have been incorrectly joined. Usually a run-on sentence has incorrect punctuation or no conjunction.

Run-on sentence: Baseball is played in the summer football is enjoyed in the fall.
Corrected punctuation: Baseball is played in the summer. Football is enjoyed in the fall.
Use of conjunction: Baseball is played in the summer, but football is enjoyed in the fall.

Read each sentence. If it is a run-on sentence, write **RO**. If the sentence is correct, write **C**.

1. In the summer, there are concerts in the park we like to take a picnic with us.   _____

2. I took my friend to a concert. We had a wonderful time.   _____

3. One concert was so crowded that we couldn't find a place to sit.   _____

4. The park is always crowded many people come to the concerts.   _____

5. The band continues to play after dark I bring a flashlight with me.   _____

Rewrite each run-on sentence as two separate sentences.

6. My friend Amanda went to every concert sometimes we would meet at the park and sit together.

_____

_____

7. Every Monday a different band would play for the eager crowd we heard a variety of music.

_____

_____

8. My family really enjoyed the jazz band the best they brought my father up on stage.

_____

_____

Correct the run-on sentences below by adding **and**, **but**, or **or**.

9. I will always remember the summer concerts ∧and the fun we had.

10. My father said he was embarrassed to go on stage he had a good time.

11. Dad likes playing the piano he doesn't like playing in front of people.

12. These are wonderful summer memories I will never forget them.

Know Your Nouns

A **common noun** is a general, or non-specific, name for a person, place, or thing.
A **proper noun** is a specific, or particular, name for the person, place, or thing.

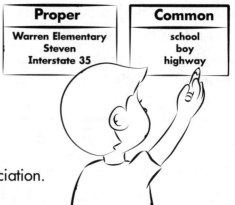

Proper	Common
Warren Elementary	school
Steven	boy
Interstate 35	highway

Sentence using common nouns:
A boy plays football for the city league.

Sentence using proper nouns:
Wesley plays for the Hornets in the Libbyville Sports Association.

Read each sentence. Write **C** for common or **P** for proper above each underlined noun.

1. Russ had always wanted to play football for the Hornets.

2. The Hornets had been an established team for many years.

3. He was very nervous the day of tryouts.

4. His father went to Ryder Field to watch Russ work his hardest.

5. Russ hoped he would do well on passes and on offensive plays.

6. Coach Reyes was amazed at Russ's talent and his ability to always find the receiver.

7. Russ and his father were very excited when Coach Reyes signed him up for the Hornets.

8. They couldn't wait to tell Wesley and his father that Russ had made the team.

Circle the common nouns and underline the proper nouns in each sentence.

9. Russ has a sister who likes to go to football games.

10. Mandy is very supportive of Russ and his desire to play football.

11. Mandy has volunteered to be a trainer for the Hornets.

12. Mandy's coach admires her support for her brother.

The Large and Small of Capitalization

The Golden Rules of Capitalization
Capitalize the following!

• Proper nouns
• The names of months, days of the week, and holidays
• The beginnings of all sentences
• Important words in titles
• Interjection words (For example: Wow! and Yippee!)

Read each sentence. Underline three times the letters that should be capitalized.

1. This july, my aunt ruth is coming to visit us in texas.

2. She lives in dodge city, kansas, and manages robinson's furniture store.

3. Each summer, my uncle todd, aunt ruth, and their dog baxter visit my family.

4. I hope they make it down for our fourth of july party.

5. We plan to go to the big billy's tons of fun amusement park in dallas.

6. My sister lacey likes to ride the big roller coaster called the mouse maze.

7. I rode this coaster last april with aaron.

8. Wow! we had so much fun!

Read the common nouns below and write two proper nouns for each one.

9. ocean ___Pacific Ocean___ ___Atlantic Ocean___

10. lake _____ _____

11. street _____ _____

12. pet _____ _____

13. state _____ _____

14. country _____ _____

15. holiday _____ _____

16. month _____ _____

Positively Possessive Nouns

They're all mine!

A **possessive noun** is a noun that shows ownership. Look at the guidelines on how to write nouns in possessive form.

singular noun	add **'s**	boy's dog
plural noun ending in **s**	add **'**	girls' dresses
plural noun not ending in **s**	add **'s**	men's suits

Read each sentence. Write **S** or **P** above each underlined possessive noun to identify it as singular or plural.

1. <u>Marla's</u> friend, Katlyn likes to go to the pet shop with her every Monday.

2. The girls became interested in rabbits at the <u>store's</u> grand opening.

3. The <u>friends'</u> mothers took them to the opening.

4. The <u>store's</u> owner was pleased to have so many people attend.

5. Marla and Katlyn rushed to the <u>rabbits'</u> hutches.

6. The young <u>ladies'</u> mothers bought each a rabbit.

7. <u>Fluffy's</u> hutch was designed and built by <u>Katlyn's</u> neighbor.

8. <u>Marla's</u> rabbit lives in her back yard with complete freedom.

Write the possessive form of each noun.

9. rabbit _____ dog _____

10. pet store _____ friend _____

11. mayor _____ veterinarian _____

12. geese _____ neighbors _____

13. canaries _____ women _____

14. girls _____ windows _____

Understanding singular and plural possessive nouns

Swinging Subject Pronouns

Subject pronouns can take the place of a noun that is the subject of the sentence. These are the only pronouns that can be used as the subject of the sentence.

Singular	Plural
I	we
you	you
he, she, it	they

Underline the **subject pronoun** in each sentence.

1. I once sang with a group for the school talent show.

2. It was a wonderful song about springtime.

3. We rehearsed several times before the big night.

4. You would have enjoyed the show.

5. It had everything from magic acts to song and dance routines.

Write a **subject pronoun** that can replace the subject in each sentence.

6. Kathy and Tom performed a jazz routine. _____

7. Kathy was nervous, but calmed down once they started. _____

8. Tom was excited to get the routine over with. _____

9. Rebecca and Katy each played beautiful piano solos. _____

10. Katy had practiced for weeks to memorize her solo. _____

11. Katy, Rebecca, and I felt it was the best show ever. _____

12. Yesterday, Steven gave Katy an article from the paper. _____

13. The newspaper had a picture of her performing her talent. _____

Identifying subject pronouns

Oh! Those Object Pronouns

Me You Him Her It Us Them

Object Pronouns can take the place of nouns.
They follow action verbs in a sentence or the words
as, **to**, **with**, **for**, and **at**.

My mother gave <u>Mary and me</u> two warm cookies.
My mother gave <u>us</u> two warm cookies.

Singular	Plural
him, her, it	us
you	you
me	them

Write an **object pronoun** that can take the place of the underlined word(s) in each sentence.

1. Steven plays after school with <u>Scott and me</u>. _____
2. Scott throws the baseball at <u>Steven</u>. _____
3. My friend borrowed a book from <u>Abbey</u>. _____
4. Abbey will return <u>the book</u> tomorrow. _____
5. Annette wrote a story for <u>Mother and me</u>. _____
6. Mother gave <u>Annette</u> a new journal. _____
7. Kendra helped Kevin with <u>his story</u>. _____
8. Kevin likes to play with <u>Kendra and Annette</u>. _____
9. Kathy wanted to play with <u>Kevin and Kendra</u>. _____

Write an **object pronoun** above the underlined word(s).

It was Mrs. Smith's class' turn to arrange for morning announcements. She wanted to

come up with something fun and unique for <u>her class</u> to try for announcements. Mrs. Smith

had <u>the class</u> write out a script for each day. She told <u>the class</u> to be creative.

James was in charge of the weather. She let <u>James</u> do the weather research

for the entire week. He decided he was going to dress as a different character each day.

It really surprised <u>the class</u> that he came up with that idea. He gave his research to

<u>Mrs. Smith</u> to check over before the announcements.

NEWS FLASH!

Tips for using I and me.

Tip #1: Always name yourself last when talking about yourself and another person.

Example: Janice and I **OR** Mark and me

Tip#2: When you're not sure whether to use I or me, read the sentence using only I or me.

Example: Sophie and I went to the library.   **OR**   Sophie and **me** went to the library.

<u>I</u> went to the library   <u>Me</u> went to the library.
Using the pronoun **I** in this sentence is correct.

Write **I** or **me** to complete each sentence.

1. Several friends and _____ decided to help out with the school paper.

2. Many articles were written by Karen and _____ .

3. Mrs. Keller likes the way that Ashley and _____ create the advertisements.

4. Bobby and _____ created an advertisement last fall.

5. Mrs. Cundiff and _____ wondered who would take over for Bobby.

6. Mrs. Keller suggested that Karen and _____ work together.

7. Mrs. Cundiff asked if Beth and _____ would like to write an article.

8. We were very excited and _____ couldn't wait to get started.

9. Our article was taken from an interview with the football coach and _____ .

10. He had many wonderful things to say about the newspaper and _____ .

11. My brother and _____ know Coach Randle well.

12. He and _____ had Coach Randle for P.E. class.

Challenge yourself!
Use a separate sheet of paper to write an essay about a friend or relative and some wonderful adventures you've had together. Use **I** and **me** in your sentences. Read your essay to your family or friends and watch them smile!

Amazing Adjectives

An **adjective** is a describing word for nouns and/or pronouns.
Adjectives are the magic of a sentence. They can put life into any sentence or story by adding details and clarity.

The boys stood on the beach.
The <u>four</u> <u>young</u> boys stood on the <u>warm</u> <u>sandy</u> beach.

Read each sentence. Underline the **adjectives**.

1. The bright radiant sun was shining on the warm wet backs of the water skiers.

2. My small family was looking forward to taking our shiny new ski boat on the clear lake.

3. It didn't appear that my youngest brother was going to try to use his brand new skis.

4. He wasn't looking forward to the busy wet day ahead of us.

5. My excited parents couldn't wait to introduce my timid brother to water skiing.

Write each word with two **adjectives** to describe it. Circle the noun.

6. lake _____   water _____

7. skier _____   day _____

8. dock _____   ride _____

9. boat _____   swimmer _____

Write your own adjectives to complete the paragraph.

It was a _____ morning for my _____ family. We were looking forward to our _____ trip to the _____ beach. My _____ sister looked for her _____ swimsuit everywhere. My _____ mother had just purchased it at the _____ store, and my _____ sister couldn't wait to wear it. After searching for what seemed like hours, we finally found it. It wasn't in my _____ sister's _____ drawers or in her _____ closet. She had tried it on _____ evening and forgot to take it off.

Celebrating with Verbs

An **action verb** tells what the subject is doing.
   My brother <u>ran</u> to the store.

A **linking verb** describes a state being.
   My brother <u>was</u> glad the store was open

Happy Verb Day

Identify the type of **verb** in each sentence.
Circle **A** if it's an action verb or **L** if it's a linking verb.

1. Janice <u>threw</u> a birthday party for her brother.   **A**   **L**

2. She <u>has</u> a thoughtful sister.   **A**   **L**

3. Her mother <u>sent</u> the invitations last Thursday.   **A**   **L**

4. Janice <u>was</u> glad all the guests could come.   **A**   **L**

5. Janice and her friend, Beth <u>had</u> prepared the party activities.   **A**   **L**

6. Her mother <u>was</u> excited everyone was on time.   **A**   **L**

Use a **linking verb** and **action verb** to complete the sentences.

had	have	is	was
eaten	enjoying	given	helping	snapping	thanking

7. Robert _____ everyone for coming.

8. Janice _____ the party as much as Robert.

9. His mother _____ pictures of the guests.

10. She _____ Robert the knife to cut the cake.

11. Janice _____ Robert with the cake.

12. The guests _____ every bit of cake.

Helpful Verbs

A **helping verb** helps the **main verb** describe the action that happened in the past, is happening in the present, or will happen in the future.

helping verb   main verb

She <u>was</u> <u>reading</u> a wonderful story.

Use the helping verbs **am**, **is**, **are**, **was**, or **were** when the main verb ends in **-ing**, or is in present tense.
Use the helping verbs **has**, **have**, or **had** when the main verb ends in **-ed**, or is in past tense.
Use the helping verb **will** when the main verb doesn't have a suffix, or is in future tense.

Read each sentence. Circle **HV** if the underlined verb is a helping verb or **MV** if it is a main verb.

1. Jean and I <u>wanted</u> to go to the city library yesterday.   **HV**   **MV**

2. We <u>were</u> looking for some good books to read.   **HV**   **MV**

3. I <u>had</u> asked my mother earlier in the morning.   **HV**   **MV**

4. My mother <u>agreed</u> to drive us to the library.   **HV**   **MV**

Circle the main verb and underline the helping verb in each sentence.

5. The librarian was putting the new books on the shelves.

6. She was listing their titles to us.

7. We were watching her stack the books.

8. Jean and I were hoping to find our favorite ones.

Use the helping verbs **am**, **are**, **has**, **have**, and **will** to complete the sentences.

9. My mother_____ take us to the library again.

10. She _____ spoken to Jean's mother.

11. They_____ pleased that we like the library.

12. I _____ excited that they have so many good books.

The Amazing Ability of Adverbs

An **adverb** describes a verb.
It tells **how**, **when**, or **where**.
Most adverbs that tell how end with **-ly**.

I have the ability to change a lifeless sentence into one with PIZZAZ!

Adverb

Write **how**, **when**, or **where** on the line
to tell how the adverb would describe a verb.

1. slowly __how__   early _____   then _____   here _____

2. sadly _____   outside _____   later _____   upstairs _____

3. inside _____   never _____   usually _____   rapidly _____

4. off _____   happily _____   there _____   now _____

Circle the adverb in each sentence.

5. Dale and I patiently waited for mother.

6. She had gone inside the hardware store.

7. Earlier, Mother had read the sale sign.

8. She quickly knew what we needed for our project.

9. We happily worked on our science project.

Underline the verb and circle the adverb in each sentence. Then circle **how**, **when**, or **where** to tell how the adverb describes the verb.

10. I presented my science project yesterday.	**how**	**when**	**where**
11. The entire class completed theirs carefully.	**how**	**when**	**where**
12. We usually hope for good grades.	**how**	**when**	**where**
13. Mrs. Gibson listened attentively to our presentations.	**how**	**when**	**where**
14. We gave the presentations in the lunchroom.	**how**	**when**	**where**

Challenge yourself!
Pretend you're a sports reporter after a big game. Write about the game using adverbs.
Use a separate piece of paper.

Cooling Off with Good and Well

Good is an adjective to describe a noun.

Lindsey is a **good** swimming instructor.

Well is an adverb used to describe a verb.

She swims **well**.

Circle **good** or **well** to complete each sentence.

1. Lindsey is (good, well) at doing the butterfly stroke.

2. She has learned to swim (good, well).

3. We learned the lesson (good, well).

4. It is hard to swim (good, well) in the ocean.

5. The sand feels (good, well) between my toes.

6. Everyone listens (good, well) to Lindsey's stories.

7. She showed my sister a (good, well) way to save others.

8. Lindsey planned her swim schedule (good, well).

9. It was (good, well) to see everyone having a good time.

10. She performed (good, well) at last week's swim meet.

Write **good** or **well** to complete each sentence.

11. My favorite dessert is ice cream, because it tastes _____.

12. I visited my grandma yesterday and she wasn't feeling _____.

13. We rested _____ at the Beach Front Hotel.

14. I did a _____ job on my science project.

Challenge yourself!
Use construction paper to create a billboard that advertises something. Be sure to use **good** and **well** on your billboard.

Understanding the usage of **good** and **well**

Preppy Prepositions

A **preposition** shows the connection between other words in a sentence.
A **prepositional phrase** starts with a preposition and ends with a noun or pronoun.

The man was working **beside** the computer.
    preposition: beside
    prepositional phrase: beside the computer

Look closely at the picture. Write a preposition to complete each sentence. Then circle the prepositional phrase. Use the list of common prepositions if you need help.

1. The computer is _____ the desk.

2. The windows are _____ the desk.

3. The paper is _____ the books.

4. The chair is _____ the desk.

5. Pens fit _____ the cup.

6. The lamp is _____ the cup of pens.

7. The printer is _____ the desk.

8. The stack _____ papers are nice and neat.

9. No one is _____ the desk.

10. The windows are _____ the computer.

11. The lamp is _____ the edge of the desk.

12. The books _____ the paper are new.

Common Prepositions	
about	above
across	after
along	at
before	behind
below	beside
by	down
during	for
from	in
inside	near
of	off
on	over
under	without

All Aboard With Abbreviations

Which words can be shortened to fit on the train better?

Texas Southern Rail Company

Cooper Paper Company

An **abbreviation** is a shortened word. Almost all abbreviations start with a capital letter and end with a period.

Words that can be abbreviated include titles, states, addresses, months, and days. Some examples of abbreviations are shown below.

Titles		Addresses		Months		Days	
Senior	**Sr.**	Street	**St.**	January	**Jan.**	Sunday	**Sun.**
Mister	**Mr.**	Road	**Rd.**	November	**Nov.**	Monday	**Mon.**
Doctor	**Dr.**	Boulevard	**Blvd.**	April	**Apr.**	Tuesday	**Tues.**
Married woman	**Mrs.**	Company	**Co.**	December	**Dec.**	Thursday	**Thurs.**
Any woman	**Ms.**	Avenue	**Ave.**	September	**Sept.**	Saturday	**Sat.**

Rewrite each group of words using an abbreviation. Use a dictionary or atlas if you need help.

November 22 _____

Doctor Beard _____

Wednesday _____

Lincoln Boulevard _____

Turtle Road _____

Northwest Company _____

Doctor Bernie _____

Saturday _____

B. Carter Junior _____

J. Smith Senior _____

Grand Circle _____

Friday _____

Sandy Boulevard _____

March 29 _____

Mister Alex Smith Senior _____

2315 Creekwood Drive _____

Mister John Clayton _____

Treats Company _____

Miami, Florida _____

Augusta, Maine _____

456 Highpark Avenue _____

February 12 _____

North Alder Street _____

Pratt Road _____

Mister Davis _____

September _____

Campus Drive _____

October 30 _____

Understanding abbreviations

A Collection of Commas

A list of three or more words in a sentence is called a **series**.
A **series** is punctuated by a comma after each word, except the last.
    "I collect **stamps**, **photos**, and **matchbooks**."
Commas also are used to separate words at the beginning of sentences, such as **yes**, **no**, and **well**.
    "**No**, I don't collect toy trains."
Commas can set off a person being addressed.
    "**Mario**, do you collect cars?"

What do you collect?

Create a list of things you collect and separate them by using commas!

Read the paragraph, adding commas where they are needed.

    Having a collection is a wonderful hobby. Collecting items such as pictures toys and music can be easy and fun. Get started by finding something you enjoy. Then read study and take notes on what you are interested in. This will help you organize your collection. Next find a special place to keep your collection. Places such as a desk drawer a cabinet or even under your bed can be good choices. Anyone can have a collection just by showing motivation imagination and creativity. Yes you can do it! So start your collection and have fun!

Rewrite each sentence correctly by adding commas where they are needed.

1. Krissy what do you know about coin collecting?

_____

2. Yes we might start a new collection of oldies music.

_____

3. Collecting things such as buttons pins and bottles can be fun.

_____

4. Well girls might collect dolls stickers and stamps.

_____

5. Boys might collect insects toy trains cars and marbles.

_____

Speak Up!

Use **quotation marks** " " at the beginning and ending of a speaker's exact words. Use a comma to separate the words being spoken from the rest of the sentence. Always place the ending punctuation inside the last quotation mark.

Kevin asked, "Debbie, did you feed Rover this evening?"

Woof!

Notice the **comma** and **question mark** placement.

Rewrite each sentence using the correct punctuation and capitalization.

1. I remember when we got Rover yelled Sally.

_____

2. Sandra asked do you remember how excited we were to take him home?

_____

3. He wanted to play all night long said Kevin

_____

4. Rover's favorite thing to do is play with Frisbees said Sally.

_____

5. Sandra exclaimed I like taking him on walks

_____

6. Wow said Kevin I can't believe we have had Rover for over five years.

_____

7. Did you do anything special with Rover today asked Debbie.

_____

8. Sally answered he rode with me to the supermarket.

_____

9. I took him to the park for a jog remarked Kevin

_____

10. Okay said Debbie he should be ready for a nap!

_____

Using quotation marks

Terrific Titles

Titles of a books, plays, movies, magazines, or newspapers are always underlined. Each important word in a title should be capitalized. ———▶ <u>The Green Grass of Ireland</u>

Titles of stories, songs, chapters, or articles are placed inside quotation marks. ———▶ "The Native Americans"

Read the sentences. Rewrite the title in each sentence correctly.

1. An article in this weeks daily times is called eating healthy.

   _____

2. Spider's design is a touching book about a spider and a dog.

   _____

3. Laughing elephants was the longest running play on Broadway.

   _____

4. Grandma read the book the night sky to me on Saturday.

   _____

Humor

Mystery

Fiction

5. My parents bought me a subscription to the kitty digest.

   _____

6. Who wrote soccer buddy and baseball billy?

   _____

   Create a title for each of these books.

7. My aunt's favorite patriotic song was the beautiful land.

   _____

8. My father's favorite movie is adventures in racing.

   _____

   Did you remember to add your punctuation?

9. I found an article for my report in the allen morning news.

   _____

10. I am also using the book polly, pioneer girl in my report.

   _____

More Ways to Dazzle Your Writing

Similes and **metaphors** are tools used in writing and speaking to compare and describe things.

A **simile** uses words **like** or **as** to make comparisons.

run **like** the wind
quick **as** as cat

As Good as Gold

A **metaphor** compares two things by saying one is the other.

His neck **is** a tree trunk, long and thick.
His legs **were** bean poles, long and round.

Underline what is being compared in each sentence. Write **simile** or **metaphor** to identify the type of comparison.

1. The snowman rose high above the land like a tall giant. _____

2. Its large eyes were dark saucers staring out into space. _____

3. His long carrot nose was stiff as a board. _____

4. The tall hat was a large crown perched upon his head. _____

5. He held a broom like a king guarding his throne. _____

Finish the **simile** to complete each sentence.

6. The weather was as cold as _____.

7. Our laughter was as loud as _____.

8. The snow fell as softly as _____.

Finish the **metaphor** to complete the sentence.

9. The hot chocolate was _____.

10. The trip home is _____.

11. Our smiles were _____.

Challenge yourself!
Write two paragraphs about a trip you took with your family on a separate sheet of paper.
Use similes and metaphors to describe what you saw or experienced on your trip.

Identifying similes and metaphors

Paint a Picture with Words

A **sentence** can tell basic information, or it can paint a picture with words.

He cut the grass.

the warm glow of sunlight

a soft snow-covered peak

the wave of the soft sweet-smelling evergreen trees

a deep flowing river

adjective   noun   adverb   verb   adjectives   tells where

The young boy quickly mowed the tall thick grass in the front yard.

Rewrite each sentence below. Use descriptive words and phrases to paint a picture with words.

1. The dog ran to the boy.

   _____

2. The girl played with the kitten.

   _____

3. Mother went to the mailbox.

   _____

4. The car's horn honked.

   _____

5. Father drove the car.

   _____

6. The girl looked at her parents.

   _____

7. They went into the house.

   _____

8. The boy and girl sat down.

   _____

Where is My Voice?

A personal narrative told from your point of view is a first person narrative. You, as the writer, will use words such as **I** and **me**.

Your speaking voice has a unique sound. Your **writing voice** is the unique way in which you express thoughts and ideas on paper. Writing with **voice** lets the reader hear the person behind the words.

A **weak voice** will sound dull:

Last summer, I went camping with my family. We had a great time. My favorite time was when we roasted marshmallows.

A **strong voice** will sound interesting:

I love camping with my family. You should see us every summer at Beaver's Bend! We have a fantastic time! The funniest memory I have is when we were roasting marshmallows and my sister jumped about a mile off the ground. She thought she saw a bear in the woods! We laughed until our stomachs hurt!

Rewrite the personal narrative below using a strong voice.

My mom told us to be back to the campsite by dark. We decided to keep hiking and find the family of hawks we heard were nearby. When we found the hawks, we got to see the three babies they had in their family. Then we turned around and headed back to the campsite. It was getting darker and darker. We had a hard time finding our way back. Finally, we arrived and my mom was mad.

_____

_____

_____

_____

_____

_____

_____

_____

Challenge yourself!
Give this paragraph a title that will grab the reader's attention. Then create a paragraph of your own using a strong voice. Use a separate sheet of paper.

Using voice in writing

Getting a Stronger Voice

Complete each step in the checklist. Use the editor's marks as you make changes.

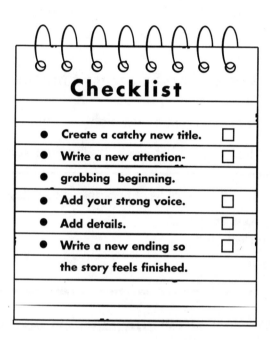

Checklist

- ● **Create a catchy new title.** ☐
- ● **Write a new attention-** ☐
- ● **grabbing beginning.**
- ● **Add your strong voice.** ☐
- ● **Add details.** ☐
- ● **Write a new ending so** ☐
- **the story feels finished.**

Proofreader/Editor's Marks

delete	ℓ
insert/add	∧
new paragraph	¶

The Night I Danced Forever

It was my cousin Cheryl's wedding. She looked beautiful in her wedding dress. It made me think of the day that I would get married. I was excited. The wedding reception was fun. Cheryl and her new husband cut the cake, took some pictures, and made a wonderful toast. I was happy to be a part of this day. After we ate it was time for the dancing. The bride and groom had their first dance. It was very special. Then everyone was invited to join in. My favorite dance was the Hokey Pokey. It was funny to see my mom dance. We danced all night long. I even got asked to dance by a boy. I was glad the song was a short one. The time came when the bride and groom left for their honeymoon. It was sad to see them go. Everyone went back out on the dance floor and danced until dawn.

Eventful Events

First Then Later Finally Meanwhile At Last

Always list events in order to keep your story organized and flowing smoothly.
Time sequence words and phrases are helpful in ordering events.

Some Time Sequence Words

first, second, next, then, last, later, before, after, finally, yesterday, today, meanwhile

Some Time Sequence Phrases

in the meantime, last night, this morning, last week, next week, by the time, later

Most stories should have at least three events. Each event should have at least two details that describe it.

Event: My sister, Ann, grabbed another long dress from the rack.
Detail #1: This was going to be the ninth dress she had tried on.
Detail #2: It looked identical to two others she's already tried.

Number the sentences in column A to put the events in order. Then number the sentences in column B to put the events in order.

A

___ Then I peddled quickly down the street.
___ Yesterday I decided to get some fresh air.
___ I took my bicycle from the garage.

B

___ Finally, I arrived at the park.
___ I passed my friend's house on the way.
___ Next, I stopped at the light to cross the street.

Read the paragraph. Circle all the time sequence words and phrases and underline the details.

Yesterday I decided to get some fresh air. It had been raining all morning and I was stuck inside with nothing to do. I took my bicycle from the garage. Its sleek colors and racing wheels seemed to be begging for a long ride. After I closed the garage door, I climbed aboard and peddled quickly down the street. Next, I passed my friend's house. I hadn't visited with Billy in a few days, but decided to continue on. By the time I stopped at the stoplight to cross the street, I could feel my heart pounding with excitement. I knew the swings would be empty and ready to soar in the air. Finally I arrived at the park. To my surprise, Billy was already sitting aboard a swing. He had been waiting for my arrival.

Organizing Your Narrative

Organized writing should:
- list events in order that they happen, using key words such as **first**, **next**, **then**, and **finally**
- tell who, what, when, where, and why (the five Ws)
- describe events through the five senses
- begin with a graphic organizer

Number the events in order from 1 to 3, then add use your imagination to add supporting details for each event.

Topic: Boating at Lake Whitney

Event #_____
Boating on the lake

_____

_____

Event #_____
Getting stuck in the rainstorm

_____

_____

Event #_____
Planning the boat trip

_____

_____

Use the graphic organizer to organize the main events and supporting details.

Topic	Main Events	Details
_____ _____ _____	1._____ _____ _____ 2._____ _____ _____ 3._____ _____ _____	_____ _____ _____ _____ _____ _____ _____ _____ _____

Challenge yourself!
On another sheet of paper, write your final copy of the boating trip to Lake Whitney.

Introductions that Explode!

Three Good Strategies for Beginning a Story

#1 — Ask a **question** to make the reader want to continue reading and find the answer.

#2 — Make a **surprising, or strong statement**.

#3 — Use **dialogue** between characters.

Use strategy #1 to write a stronger beginning sentence for this paragraph.

<u>My puppy had made a mess in the kitchen</u>. I saw the plant leaves and stems scattered everywhere. Soil was spread across the kitchen floor. The planters, with dirt still clinging to them, were on their sides. I thought what monster could have been so cruel to these helpless plants. Then I saw my innocent little puppy standing to the side of the mess.

1. _____

Use strategy #2 to write a stronger beginning sentence for this paragraph.

<u>I was lost in the mall once</u>. When I looked around I didn't see a person I knew. It was like being in a foreign country, and I didn't speak the language. My mother had been with me just a second ago, and had now vanished. I thought about yelling for help, when I realized that going up to the sales lady might work. She informed me that my mother had just stepped into the dressing room with a stack of clothes. I could feel the relief in my stomach.

2. _____

Use strategy #3 to write a stronger beginning sentence for this paragraph.

<u>We had a flat tire on vacation</u>. We were on our way back from my grandmother's house when a noise, like a loud fire cracker broke through the car. My mother, who was dozing at the time jumped with fright. My father quickly pulled the car to the side of the rode and set about changing the tire. I was honored when he asked me to assist him.

3. _____

Challenge yourself!

Write introductions for the following story topics using the strategies for dynamic introductions: the first day of school, playing your favorite game with a friend, and a rainy day. Use a separate sheet of paper.

Writing an introduction

Wrap It Up!

A good ending wraps up loose ends.

Tips for Ending a Story

• Tell the reader how the events worked out.
• Express your (the author's) feelings and thoughts about the experience.
• Use elaboration and details to enhance the ending.

WEAK ENDING
We fixed the tire and were on our way.

STRONG ENDING
Almost like a magician, my father zapped the the spare tire into place. We were soon on our way, hoping my father wouldn't have to work anymore "magic" on this trip.

Pretend you have written a story about each topic below and write a strong ending.

1. My dog was lost and I just found him.

_____

_____

2. I accidentally spilled paint all over my mom's new carpet.

_____

_____

3. It was the first time I had ever been on the roller coaster.

_____

_____

4. My friend's talked me into visiting a haunted house.

_____

_____

5. It was the best day ever.

_____

_____

Challenge yourself!
Gather up some of your favorite books by your favorite authors. Read their strong endings for the chapters and the entire story. Then try to write your own. Use a separate sheet of paper.

Building A Story

Build the perfect story.
Use the checklist below for help.

Checklist for Building a Strong Story

- Choose your topic ❑

- Decide who is telling the story? Yourself? Another character? A group of characters? ❑

- Decide on your purpose. Will the story be funny? Serious? Informative? ❑

- Decide whom you are writing the story for. Who are your intended readers? ❑

Using the prompt below, write a personal narrative on the lines provided. If you need more room, use a piece of notebook paper to continue your story.

Your family and you are on vacation. It is late at night, and there is only one place left to stay...the manor at the edge of town. Watch out! It might be haunted. Write about your adventure.

_____

_____

_____

_____

_____

_____

_____

_____

Writing a personal narrative

A Handy "How To"

An **informative narrative** or **"how to"** is
a composition telling how to do something.

Handy Tips for Writing an Informative "How To"

What's Your Purpose and Who's Your Reader?

1st: Introduction – This may be an interesting statement or question
about the main idea.

2nd: Materials – List all the materials that are needed. This needs to be in an interesting sentence.

3rd: Order of Steps – Write all the steps needed in correct order. Use proper sequencing words.

4th: Details – Make sure to use exact details to make your steps clear. Use examples and reasons
or completing each step.

5th: Conclusion – End your "how to" with a strong closing sentence.

Write a composition on how to make an ice cream sundae.

Introduction: _____

_____

First: _____

_____

Second: _____

_____

Next: _____

_____

Then: _____

_____

Finally: _____

_____

Conclusion: _____

The Power of Persuasion

An **informative persuasion** or **persuasive descriptive** states and supports a position or opinion.

Tips for Writing a Powerful Informative Persuasion
What's Your Purpose and Who's Your Reader?

1st: Introduction – Using a strong beginning, state your position or opinion. You may list your reasons, but do not explain them in this paragraph.

2nd: Reasons – List at least three reasons. Tell why and give examples.

3rd: Conclusion – Re-state your opinion and tie up loose ends. Make a statement.

Your teacher has instilled a policy that allows students to work through their recess, if they so choose. This allows those students to work ahead in their studies. Use the model below to write a persuasive composition, explaining why you agree with the policy or why you do not.

Introduction: _____

_____

Reason 1: _____

_____

Reason 2: _____

_____

Reason 3: _____

_____

Conclusion: _____

_____

Ups and Downs

An **informative classificatory**
compares and contracts two things.

Tips for Writing an Informative Classificatory
Think about Your Purpose and Your Reader

1st: Introduction – Write a strong introduction that tells briefly about the topic.

2nd: Opinion #1 – State what you like about the topic. Give at least three examples and back up your opinions with details. Ask yourself "why?"

3rd: Opinion #2 – State what you don't like about your topic. Give at least three examples and back up your opinions with details. Ask yourself "why?"

4th: Conclusion – Write a strong conclusion that sums up the important points and ties up loose ends.

Your mother wants to buy you a pet. Use the model below to write a composition explaining what is both good and bad about owning a pet.

Introduction: _____

_____

Opinion #1: _____

_____

_____

Opinion #2: _____

_____

_____

Conclusion: _____

_____

Writing a Friendly Letter

A **friendly letter** has four parts:

(1) Greeting – which begins with Dear and is followed by the receiver's name and a comma.

(2) Body – which is the main part of the letter.

(3) Closing – which finishes the letter and is followed by a comma.

(4) Signature – which tells who wrote the letter.

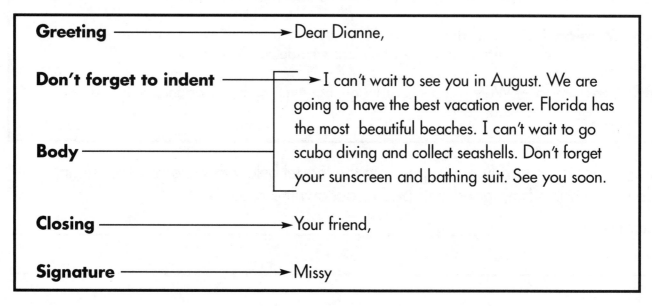

Greeting ──────────────→ Dear Dianne,

Don't forget to indent ──────┐

Body ───────────────── → I can't wait to see you in August. We are going to have the best vacation ever. Florida has the most beautiful beaches. I can't wait to go scuba diving and collect seashells. Don't forget your sunscreen and bathing suit. See you soon.

Closing ──────────────→ Your friend,

Signature ─────────────→ Missy

Write a friendly letter to a friend or relative to let them know your plans for your next vacation.

_____

_____

_____

_____

_____

_____

ABC . . . 123

Rewrite each set of words in alphabetical order.

1.

wither   _____

remorse   _____

bizarre   _____

built   _____

realm   _____

wilt   _____

2.

gorge   _____

waddle   _____

golden   _____

utter   _____

gallon   _____

ward   _____

3.

function _____

fruitful _____

fudge   _____

freight   _____

fumble   _____

fumigate _____

4.

sleazy   _____

slicker   _____

slide   _____

sleepily _____

slight   _____

slipper   _____

Dictionary Fun

Two **guide words** are shown at the top of each page of the dictionary. The first guide word is the first word on that page, and the second is the last. The other words on the page will be in alphabetical order between the two guide words.

Example: If the guide words are **sorrow** and **southwest**, then other words on that page will include **sorry**, **sound**, **soul**, **sound**, **soup**, **sour**, and **south**.

Guide words with page numbers are shown for an imaginary dictionary. Use the information to write the page numbers where you would find the following words in this imaginary dictionary.

fullback	259	**fur**

furbish	260	**fuzzy**

gab	261	**galaxy**

gale	262	**game**

1. gallop _____   further _____   fumble _____

2. galley _____   gable _____   future _____

3. fume _____   fun _____   gain _____

4. fussy _____   fury _____   gallery _____

5. gallant _____   fullness _____   fungus _____

6. funnel _____   gain _____   further _____

7. fusion _____   galore _____   gallon _____

8. gallery _____   furnace _____   future _____

9. gala _____   fuse _____   galaxy _____

10. gaggle _____   function _____   funeral _____

11. fuzz _____   gait _____   gadget _____

12. gall _____   gab _____   futile _____

Using guide words; dictionary skills

What Part is What?

A **full title page** is found at the front of the book and tells the title, author, and publisher of the book.

A **copyright information** is located on the back of the title page. It tells you the year in which the book was published.

A **table of contents** comes after the copyright page and shows the book's chapters and on which page each begins.

An **index** is found at the back of the book. It lists all the book's topics in alphabetical order and shows on which page or pages each topic is mentioned.

A **glossary** is sometimes found in the back of the book. It provides definitions of words you need to understand throughout the book.

Write the part of a book that would be used to answer each question.

1. Does the book have any information on low fat foods? _____

2. Who is the author? _____

3. On what page does Chapter 7 begin? _____

4. What kind of pan is a jelly-roll pan? _____

5. How up to date are the recipes in this book? _____

6. Who is the publisher of the book? _____

7. Which pages tell about easy bake chicken and pasta? _____

8. What is the title of Chapter 3? _____

9. Is there a chapter on easy 20-minute dishes? _____

10. What year was this book published? _____

It's a Hard Rock Life

Chapters are listed in order ⟶

The page on which a chapter begins

Table of Contents

Use the table of contents above to answer each question.

1. Which chapter would discuss amethysts and other crystals? _____

2. How many pages are there in the chapter on Jewelry and Bead Making? _____

3. What kinds of things might Chapter 6 contain?

    _____

4. Which chapter might list places to look for gold? _____

5. How many chapters are in this book? _____

6. What might be a title for this book?

    _____

7. How many pages are in Chapter 1? _____

8. In which chapter would you learn how to crimp beads? _____

9. In which chapter would you find advice on helping a sprained ankle naturally? _____

10. Name some things on which you would find information in Chapter 1.

    _____

11. If you could add a Chapter 7 what might it be called?

    _____

12. How is this book organized?

    _____

Index Intelligence

Civil War

amputations 53		Davis, Jefferson 32	
battles 29-32, 36-42, 50-53		Fort Sumter 37-38	
battle ships 23-24			
Blue, the 5		generals 30-31	
		Gettysburg 50-53	
Bull Run 39		Grant, Ulysses S. 30	
carpetbaggers 44		hospitals 53-54	
Confederacy 5			
		Lee, Robert E. 31	

Above is a portion of an index from a book about the Civil War.
Write the page numbers below to answer the questions.

1. Which page or pages will contain information about:

   carpetbaggers _____   hospitals _____

   battles _____   Fort Sumter _____

   amputations _____   Jefferson Davis _____

2. After looking at the index, what do you think Gettysburg, Bull Run, and battles have in common?

   _____

3. After looking at the index, what do you think Ulysses S. Grant and Robert E. Lee had in common?

   _____

4. What pages do you think you would look at to find out about battles fought in the ocean?

   _____

5. After looking at the index, what do you think was a possible result of an injury received in the Civil War?

   _____

6. Would you find information about carpetbaggers on
   pages before or after information about the hospitals? _____

7. After looking at the index, what color do you think the Confederacy was nicknamed? _____

Let the Fireworks Begin!

Helpful Hints to Better Reading Comprehension:

- Read the questions first.
- Read once for enjoyment and twice for information.
- Underline the title and number the paragraphs.
- Highlight all bold print words.

Before reading this story and the story on page 47, review the questions about them on pages 48-50.

One scorching hot summer afternoon, we ventured down Main Street to fight the crowd as we watched the parade. It was the Fourth of July! We had waited for this day all year. Not bothered by the heat of the day, we watched the parade that **extended** like a snake down several city blocks. The parade included fire trucks, old cars, and decorated floats from the local stores. It was pretty much the same every year, but we didn't care because it was the parade, and candy was to be thrown from the floats. We knew by the end of this event we'd have bushels and bushels of candy in our possession.

After the parade, my family and I headed back to my uncle's house for a barbeque with my relatives. The first question from my little sister was, "When is the sky going to show us its sparkles?" She believes that fireworks come naturally from above. I hesitated to tell her that fireworks are not born in the sky, but are **launched** with a machine by our local fire department. We waited anxiously as the sun set below the trees. It seemed like it took forever. My sister yelled out every so often, "Isn't it time yet?" She has no patience when it comes to fireworks.

Finally, it was time and as always my parents packed the car with lawn chairs and coolers. We headed out to an empty parking lot to get a closer view. The fireworks began to boom and explode as fast as lightening hitting the sky.

In no time at all, the firework show was over and another Fourth of July had passed. It seemed like the day had just started and then was only a memory. I wonder how this fun day got started?

Applying reading skills; fiction passage

The History of the Fourth of July

Independence Day, also known as the Fourth of July, is a national holiday of the United States of America. Like Christmas, it is a time that families get together. They enjoy barbeques, picnics, and parades.

July 4th, 1776 was the date that the Declaration of Independence was signed by the Continental Congress in Philadelphia. However, Congress did not finally **establish** the Fourth of July as a legal holiday until 1941.

At the time of the signing, the United States consisted of thirteen colonies, under the rule of England's King George III. The public **cry** argued the fairness of the thirteen colonies in America being forced to pay taxes to the King of England. This practice was referred to as Taxation Without Representation. The **unrest** grew in the colonies, so King George sent troops to help control the situation. In 1774, the thirteen colonies sent delegates to Philadelphia to form the First Continental Congress. For an entire year, the Congress tried to work out the colonists' differences with England.

By June 1776 a committee was formed to **compose** the Declaration of Independence. The committee was headed by Thomas Jefferson. After many changes to the writing of the document, a vote for its signing was taken on July 4th late in the afternoon. John Hancock, President of the Continental Congress, was the first to sign the Declaration of Independence. Although the signing of the Declaration was not completed until August, the Fourth of July is the official anniversary.

Reading Comprehension I

Answer the following questions about "Let the Fireworks Begin!" on page 46.

Context Clues

1. Write the definition for the word **extended**. Then write a sentence using the word.

   _____

   _____

2. Write the definition for the word **launched**. Then write a sentence using the word.

   _____

   _____

3. Number the following sentences in the order they happened in the story.

   _____ My family and I headed back for a barbeque.

   _____ We had bushels and bushels of candy.

   _____ We watched the parade that extending like a snake down several city blocks.

   _____ The firework show was over and another Fourth of July had passed.

   _____ Fireworks are launched with a machine by our local fire department.

Drawing Conclusions

4. Describe the younger sister's personality. _____

5. Explain what the older sister meant when she said, "Fireworks are not born in the sky."

   _____

6. List specific words or quotes from the story that explain the writer's feelings about this holiday.

   _____

Similes

7. Write a simile contained in the story. _____

8. Write a new simile to use in the story. _____

Applying reading skills

Reading Comprehension II

Answer the following questions about "The History of the Fourth of July" on page 47. Fill in the circle next to the correct answer.

1. What is the main idea of paragraph 3?
    - ○ a. The struggle between the United States and England.
    - ○ b. The ruling of King George III
    - ○ c. How Americans Celebrate the Fourth of July
    - ○ d. King George III sending troops to help control the fight

2. In paragraph 2, what does the word **establish** mean?
    - ○ a. to withdraw
    - ○ b. to set up
    - ○ c. to consider
    - ○ d. to hold

3. In paragraph 3, what does the word **cry** mean?
    - ○ a. to laugh
    - ○ b. to shout
    - ○ c. to bawl
    - ○ d. to forget

4. In paragraph 3, what does the word **unrest** mean?
    - ○ a. to not sleep
    - ○ b. to be forceful
    - ○ c. to cover
    - ○ d. to have anxiety

5. In paragraph 4, what does the word **compose** mean?
    - ○ a. to create
    - ○ b. to make calm
    - ○ c. to make agitated
    - ○ d. to ignore

6. What happened after the committee was formed in 1776?
    - ○ a. John Hancock signed the Declaration of Independence.
    - ○ b. The United States went to war.
    - ○ c. The Declaration of Independence was formed.
    - ○ d. King George III brings in his troops.

7. What happened in the year 1941?
    - ○ a. The Declaration of Independence was signed.
    - ○ b. John Hancock became President of the Continental Congress.
    - ○ c. Congress set the Fourth of July as a legal holiday.
    - ○ d. Taxation Without Representation became effective.

8. What was the effect of the committee that was formed in 1776?
    - ○ a. The Declaration of Independence
    - ○ b. King George III
    - ○ c. Thomas Jefferson heads a committee
    - ○ d. The Fourth of July

9. What does Taxation Without Representation mean?
    - ○ a. to rebel
    - ○ b. to buy without permission
    - ○ c. to be forced to pay taxes
    - ○ d. to celebrate the Fourth of July

10. Where was the Declaration of Independence signed?
    - ○ a. Philadelphia
    - ○ b. England
    - ○ c. Texas
    - ○ d. New York

Venn Diagrams

A **Venn Diagram** organizes the similarities and differences between two things. The circles show differences. The overlapping area of the circles show similarities.

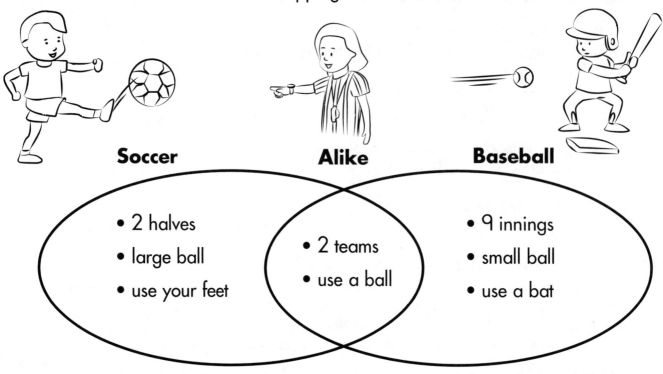

Create a **Venn Diagram** to compare "The History of the Fourth of July" and "Let the Fireworks Begin!"

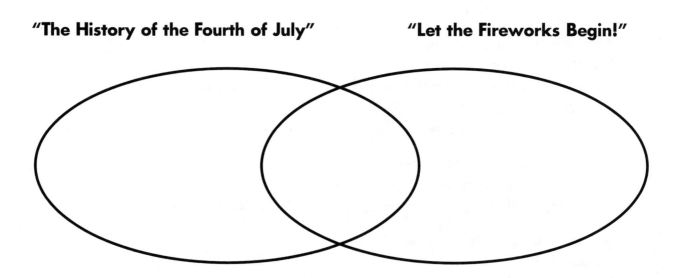

Challenge yourself!
On a separate sheet of paper, create your own comparison of things using a Venn Diagram.

Synonym and Antonym Review

Read the paragraph. Write a synonym above the underlined words.
Write an antonym above the words in bold.

To: Molly
From: Carol
Subject: Texas Snowstorm

I wish you had been in town when it snowed. It never snows in Texas. However,

the snow was not shy about coming to Texas this year. It started in the early **morning**

with <u>cold</u> rain and then by mid **morning** it began to turn to snow. The snow fell

so <u>beautifully</u>. It started off slow but then began to fall <u>more rapidly</u>. The best thing

was that school was <u>cancelled</u>. It was going to be a <u>great</u> day!

First, we went outside and <u>made</u> snow angels. Christy **hated** the way the ice

felt on her back. She wanted to stay <u>inside</u> all day.

After we had enough of the snow, we decided to go inside to drink <u>warm</u> chocolate

and roast marshmallows. We played games and baked banana bread the <u>reminder</u> of the day.

The next **evening** I made a wish that we would have another snow day. This time I

found a <u>huge</u> hill to go sledding down. (And I knew I **shouldn't** invite Christy again since

she was so <u>grumpy</u> yesterday!) Having snow days is <u>unforgettable</u>. I wish it snowed

everyday in Texas!

Word Usage

Circle the homophone(s) that correctly completes each sentence.

1. (Its, It's) a beautiful day to go and shop for a clothing (sail, sale).

2. First, (meet, meat) my (aunt, ant) and I for lunch by the (sea, see).

3. I will be wearing a pink (beau, bow) in my (hair, hare).

4. After lunch we can walk on the (beach, beech) and look for shells.

5. Then (aisle, I'll) be ready to shop!

Write the contraction for each pair of words.

6. I have _____ 　　7. I will _____

8. we are _____ 　　9. she is _____

10. they have _____ 　11. it is _____

12. do not _____ 　　13. he would _____

14. have not _____ 　15. she would _____

Circle the compound word(s) in each sentence.

16. We can take you back to the airport after lunch.

17. I will meet up with my playgroup after the airport.

18. The afternoon sun made us tired.

19. Go upstairs and get the beanbag chair for us to sit on.

20. Later we will go to the supermarket for groceries.

Language Awareness Review

Add the prefix **dis-**, **pre-**, **mis-**, **re-**, or **un-** to each word.

1. _____advantage   _____pay   _____mix

2. _____approve   _____able   _____wind

3. _____guide   _____read   _____arrange

Add the suffix **-ful**, **-ly**, or **-able** to each word.

4. grace_____   swift_____   hand_____

5. hard_____   mad_____   love_____

6. smooth_____   friend_____   suspense_____

Label each sentence as **declarative**, **interrogative**, **imperative**, or **exclamatory**.

7. Who was the 16th president of the United States?   _____

8. Please type your report on the U.S. Presidents.   _____

9. What a wonderful leader George Washington was!   _____

10. I enjoy learning about the presidents.   _____

Read the paragraph and correct all spelling, puncuation, and capitalization errors.

Lacey and Jennifer are on the south lake cross country team. Their dedicated runners who wake every morning at 600 am to rush to school to work out with the team! They run three to for miles over a variety of cross country trails. This prepairs them for the different courses they might run in a competition. In the fall season there are a competition each Saturday at rambler park in kingman. Lacey and jennifer watch what they eat the night before the big race and they make sure thay get a good nights rest. The average trail that the girls will run is two miles? Coach cleaver is proud of they're dedication to the team.

Sentence Structure Review

Circle the subject and underline the predicate in each sentence.

1. I enjoy learning more about our nation's leader.

2. George Washington was a wonderful leader.

3. Thomas Jefferson is my favorite president.

4. I wrote a report about President George Bush.

5. We showed illustrations with our report.

Rewrite each run-on sentence to form one correct sentence using conjuctions.

6. My mother's parents like to visit us in the summer my father's parents like to visit in the winter.

_____

_____

7. I wanted to ask my mother why they didn't visit at the same time my brother told me why.

_____

_____

8. My mother's parents live in the southern states my father's parents live in the northern states.

_____

_____

Rewrite each pair of sentences using a conjunction to make a compound sentence.

9. The president leads our country. He makes decisions about our nation.

_____

_____

10. When it was first built, the White House didn't have electricity. It did have an abundance of candlesticks.

_____

_____

Noun Review

Circle the proper nouns and underline the common nouns in each sentence.

1. The United States started with thirteen colonies.

2. Massachusetts, Connecticut, Rhode Island, and New Hampshire were the New England colonies.

3. Much of our nation's history took place in Boston, Massachusetts.

4. There was a famous tea party held in the Boston Harbor.

5. The water was swimming with tea.

Write the possessive form of each noun.

6. soldiers _____

7. nation _____

8. flag _____

9. horse _____

10. men _____

11. battleships _____

12. dog _____

13. fish _____

Read each sentence. Underline three times the letters that need to be capitalized.

14. the american revolution was fought between britain and the colonies.

15. george washington was a commander in the american revolution.

16. many famous men signed the declaration of independence.

17. john hancock enjoyed signing his name to this memorable document.

18. today we celebrate the fourth of july.

Nouns, Pronouns, and Adjectives

Underline the subject in each sentence. Write a subject pronoun that can replace it.

1. Tara and I are going to the Westside Mall tomorrow. _____

2. Susan and Toby will be at the movie by 7:00 p.m. _____

3. Carter and Tom are going to meet us there. _____

4. Susan and I are hoping to see a fun new adventure. _____

5. Tara wants to pay for the snacks. _____

Read each sentence. Circle the adjectives.

6. Mary and I are going to the miniature golf course.

7. Ed and Mark like to play miniature golf with Phil.

8. Phil goes to the putting green with Ed and Mark.

9. The girls like to play on the bumper boats with Shannon.

10. Terry also likes to ride small racing cars.

Read each sentence. Circle the common noun and underline the adjective(s).

11. The thrilling ride was finally over after three long minutes.

12. The bright red car went the fastest through the dark tunnel.

13. Cheri drove the bright yellow car to the top of the grassy hill.

14. Mary's small car was not very fast so she took the big blue bus.

15. Phil passed the three cars quickly to finish first in the race.

Verb Review

Write **V (verb)**, **A (adverb)**, or **HV (helping verb)** to identify each of the underlined words.

1. Grandpa and Grandma Davis <u>quickly</u> <u>pulled</u> their RV into the driveway.

2. My brother and I <u>excitedly</u> <u>rushed</u> out to meet them.

3. They <u>laughed</u> <u>loudly</u> as they opened the door.

4. My mother <u>ran</u> from <u>inside</u>.

5. She <u>had</u> <u>waited</u> <u>impatiently</u> for their arrival.

6. They <u>were</u> <u>happily</u> <u>staying</u> with us for two weeks.

7. They <u>usually</u> <u>have</u> gifts for us.

8. I <u>yelled</u> <u>loudly</u> for my father.

9. He <u>was</u> <u>upstairs</u> <u>shaving</u>.

10. He <u>trotted</u> <u>downstairs</u> to greet them.

Read the paragraph and circle the answer that best completes each sentence.

Amanda moved to Hampton three months ago. _____11._____ became best friends

immediately. She is an avid sports fan and _____12._____ attending soccer games. We met

when I was _____13._____ an indoor soccer game at the Hampton Sports Complex.

11. a. Her and I
    b. She and me
    c. She and I
    d. Me and Her

12. a. enjoying
    b. enjoys
    c. enjoyed
    d. enjoy

13. a. played
    b. plays
    c. playing
    d. play

0000r

Mixed Language Review I

Read each sentence. Circle **C** if good or well are used **correctly**. Circle **I** if they are used incorrectly.

1. I listened well.	**C**	**I**
2. He played baseball good.	**C**	**I**
3. The trip to South Carolina went good.	**C**	**I**
4. The trips we take together are good.	**C**	**I**
5. She is a good driver.	**C**	**I**

Read each sentence. Rewrite each title correctly.

6. My mother is reading the wild rabbit.

_____

7. Leah Gibson is the author of tales of my rabbit.

_____

8. I loved the article on "healthy living" in yesterday's newspaper.

_____

9. Kristi Densmore was the star of the dancing princess on Broadway.

_____

Correctly write a made-up or real title to complete each sentence.

10. _____ is a collection of mystery stories.

11. Read the book _____ to learn how to fry chicken.

12. The _____ is a newspaper everyone can enjoy.

13. Learn about current music in the magazine _____ .

14. I enjoy reading the book _____ because it is a love story.

Reviewing the usage of **good** and **well** and titles

Mixed Language Review II

Rewrite each sentence using the correct punctuation.

1. When I grow up I want to be an astronaut yelled Tim.

_____

_____

2. Craig yelled You always change your mind about what you want to be when you grow up.

_____

_____

3. I just want to be a fireman astronaut and policeman explained Tim.

_____

_____

4. Maybe you could work for NASA said Donnie.

_____

_____

5. Did you know that the stars sometimes form pictures of birds ducks and cars asked Tim.

_____

_____

Write the following using the correct abreviations.

6. Red Boulevard _____   Flame Leaf Circle _____

7. October _____   Rob Smith Senior _____

8. Oak Street _____   Mister Williams _____

9. Monday _____   November 13 _____

Write each group of words in alphabetical order.

10. encounter   enamel   emphasize   encourage   employee   empty

_____

11. circuit   cinema   chunk   chubby   church   chow   circle

_____

Writing Review

Identify the underlined words as a **metaphor** or a **simile**.

1. The United States was a <u>young baby of a country</u>. _____

2. The colonists were <u>as brave as lions</u>. _____

3. The war between the colonists and Great Britian was <u>like Jack and the giant from the beanstock</u>. _____

4. The battle ground <u>was an ant field of soldiers</u>. _____

5. The soldiers' uniforms looked <u>like a tuxedo for a dance</u>. _____

Rewrite the paragraph in a strong voice.

      Once we gave my sister a surprise birthday party. My dad had to take her out for a quick errand so we could get the guests in the door. There were so many people at the party anxiously waiting for my sister to arrive. The door began to open and we all jumped out and yelled surprise. Little did we know it was just my grandmother arriving late to the party. Finally, we all got in our places and waited to yell surprise.

_____

_____

_____

_____

_____

_____

_____

_____

Reviewing metaphors, similes, and voice

Answer Key

Please take time to review the work your child has completed and remember to praise both success and effort. If your child makes a mistake, let him or her know that mistakes are apart of learning. Then explain the correct answer and how to find it. Taking the time to help your child and an active interest in his or her progress shows that you feel learning is important.

Page 1
1. enjoyable
2. freezing
3. observed
4. journeyed
5. drowsy
6. dashed
7. thrilled, desired
8. greatest
9. whole
10. overwhelmed
Challenge yourself: Answers will vary.

Page 2
1. early
2. ended
3. lost
4. sad
5. dirty
6. liked
7. clear
8. little
9. destroy
10. night
11. late
12. sick
13. dull

Page 3
1. week
2. bawl
3. ate
4. hour
5. blew
6. where
7. aunt
8. hear
9. role
10. know
11. their
12. bear
13. deer
14. It's
Challenge yourself: Answers will vary.

Page 4
1. airplane
2. pillowcase
3. seashell
4. earthquake
5. horseshoe
6. flashlight
7. grandmother
8. brotherhood
9. boathouse
10. armchair
11. basketball
12. shoelace
Compound words in the paragraph are: baseball, weekend, daydreams, baseball, cheerleader, dugout, butterflies, hotdogs, watermelon, outside, backyard
Challenge yourself: Drawings will vary.

Page 5
1. isn't
2. can't
3. haven't
4. he'll
5. wouldn't
6. They'll
7. shouldn't, you've
8. he'll, couldn't
9. I'm, they'll
10. isn't, there'll
11. wasn't, hasn't
12. don't, aren't
13. won't, I'll
14. they're, she'll
15. he's, she's
Challenge yourself: Answers will vary.

Page 6
1. pre-/before
2. un-/not
3. re-/again, back
4. dis-/from, take away from
5. mis-/wrong
6. anti-/against
7. de-/opposite of
8. semi-/half
9. disappear, prepaid
10. misspelled, unpleasant
11. reconsider, inseparable
Words with prefixes in the paragraphs are: unbelievable, uncomfortable, prepared, preview, disappear

Page 7
1. -able/having, being that
2. -ful/full of, having those qualities
3. -less/without
4. -y/worthy of or able to
5. -ly/in a certain way
6. -ment/result of
7. -er/doer
8. -est/superlative
9. -ness/state of being
10. -ist/one who believes or does something
11. organizer, smallest
12. movement, famous
13. likeness, hopeful
Words with suffixes in the paragraphs are: violinist, beautifully, enjoyable, harpist, professionally, successful

Page 8
1. exclamatory
2. interrogative
3. declarative
4. exclamatory
5. imperative
6. interragotive
(Answers for 7-10 may vary.)
7. The fields of wheat look like oceans of gold!
8. There are different kinds of large equipment used to harvest the wheat.
9. How long has my father been harvesting wheat?
10. Finish the harvest before bad weather arrives.

Page 9
1. (Shelby) enjoys working at the family pet store.
2. (She) has many chores and duties to fulfill.
3. (The small puppies) are held on a daily basis.
4. (The kittens) like to have all the attention.
5. (Shelby) likes to help out in any way.
6. (This young girl) likes to earn her allowance.

7. CS
8. CP
9. CS
10. CP
11. CS
12. CP
13. CS, CP
14. CP

Page 10
1. S
2. C
3. S
4. S
5. C
6. C
7. My family shopped for skiing supplies, but we all didn't find what we needed.
8. My brother found the gloves he liked, and he found the suit he wanted.
9. The suit was bright red, and it had racing stripes.
10. My brother thought he might buy it, or he could use his old suit another year.
11. He wanted to buy the gloves, too, but the store didn't have them in his size.

Page 11
1. RO
2. C
3. C
4. RO
5. RO
6. My friend Amanda went to every concert. Sometimes we would meet at the park and sit together.
7. Every Monday a different band would play for the eager crowd. We heard a variety of music.
8. My family really enjoyed the jazz band the best. They brought my father up on stage.
9. I will always remember the summer concerts and the fun we had.
10. My father said he was embarrassed to go on stage but he had a good time.
11. Dad likes playing the piano but he doesn't like playing in front of people.
12. These are wonderful summer memories and I will never forget them.

Page 12

1. Russ (P), football (C), Hornets (P)
2. Hornets (PP), team (C), years (C)
3. He (C), day (C), tryouts (C)
4. father (C), Ryder Field (P), Russ (P)
5. Russ (P), he (C), passes (C), plays (C)
6. Coach Reyes (P), talent (C), ability (C), reciever (C)
7. Russ (P), father (C), Coach Reyes (P), Hornets (P)
8. They (C), Wesley (P), father (C), Russ (P), team (C)
9. Russ has a (sister) who likes to go to football (games)
10. Mandy is very supportive of Russ and his (desire) to play (football)
11. Mandy has volunteered to be a (trainer) for the Hornets.
12. Mandy's (coach) admires her (support) for her (brother)

Page 13

1. July, Aunt Ruth, Texas
2. She, Dodge City, Kansas, Robinson's Furniture Store
3. Uncle Todd, Aunt Ruth, Baxter
4. I, Fourth of July
5. We, Big Billy's Tons of Fun Amusement Park, Dallas
6. Lacey, Mouse Maze
7. April, Aaron
8. Wow, We

(Answers for 9-16 may vary.)

9. Pacific Ocean, Atlantic Ocean
10. Lake Texahoma, Lake Superior
11. Pine Street, Elm Street
12. Fluffy, Emma
13. Texas, Michigan
14. Africa, United States
15. Christmas, Easter
16. October, November

Page 14

1. S
2. S
3. P
4. S
5. P
6. P
7. S, S
8. S
9. rabbit's, dog's
10. pet store's, friend's
11. mayor's, veterinarian's
12. geese's, neighbors'
13. canaries', women's
14. girls', windows'

Page 15

1. I
2. It
3. We
4. You
5. It
6. They
7. She
8. He
9. They
10. She
11. We
12. He
13. It

Page 16

1. us
2. him
3. her
4. it
5. us
6. her
7. it
8. them
9. them

Object pronouns for the paragraphs are:
them (her class), them (the class), them (the class), him (James), them (the class), her (Mrs. Smith)

Page 17

1. I
2. me
3. I
4. I
5. I
6. I
7. I
8. I
9. me
10. me
11. I
12. I

Challenge yourself: Answers will vary.

Page 18

1. bright, radiant, warm, water
2. small, shiny, new, clear,
3. youngest, brand, new,
4. busy, wet
5. excited, timid, water

(Answers for 6-9 will vary.)

6. clear blue (lake), cool crisp (water)
7. skillful young (skier) long hot (day)
8. old wooden (dock) long wet (ride)
9. small speedy (boat) timid young (swimmer)

Adjectives for the paragraph will vary. Possible answers are: busy morning, eager family, long trip, sunny beach, big sister, yellow swimsuit, generous mother, clothing store, impatient sister, silly sister's, dresser drawers, bedroom closet, yesterday evening

Page 19

1. A
2. L
3. A
4. L
5. L
6. L
7. was thanking
8. was enjoying
9. is snapping
10. had given
11. was helping
12. have eaten

(Answers for 7-12 may vary.)

Page 20

1. MV
2. HV
3. HV
4. MV
5. The librarian was (putting) the new books on the shelves.
6. She was (listing) their titles to us.
7. We were (watching) her stack the books.
8. Jean and I were (hoping) to find our favorite ones.
9. will
10. has
11. are
12. am

Page 21

1. how, when, when, where
2. how, where, when, where
3. where, when, when, how
4. where, how, where, when
5. patiently
6. inside
7. Earlier
8. quickly
9. happily
10. presented (yesterday), when
11. completed (carefully), how
12. (usually) hope, when
13. listened (attentively), how
14. gave (in), where

Challenge yourself: Answers will vary.

Page 22

1. good
2. well
3. well
4. well
5. good
6. well
7. good
8. well
9. good
10. well
11. good
12. well
13. well
14. good

Challenge yourself: Answers will vary.

Page 23

Answers may vary.

1. on the desk
2. above the desk
3. near the books
4. under the desk
5. in the cup
6. near the cup
7. beside the desk
8. of papers
9. at the desk
10. behind the computer
11. on the edge
12. by the papers

Page 24

Nov. 22	Mr. Alex Smith Sr.
Dr. Beard	2315 Creekwood Dr.
Wed.	Mr. John Clayton
Lincoln Blvd.	Treats Co.
Turtle Rd.	Miami, Fl.
Northwest Co.	Augusta, Me.
Dr. Bernie	456 Highpark Ave.
Sat.	Feb. 12
B. Carter Jr.	N. Alder St.
J. Smith Sr.	Pratt Rd.
Grand Cr.	Mr. Davis
Fri.	Sept.
Sandy Blvd.	Campus Dr.
Mar. 29	Oct. 30

Page 25

Having a collection is a wonderful hobby. Collecting items such as pictures, toys, and music can be easy and fun. Get started by finding something you enjoy. Then read, study, and take notes on what you are interested in. This will help you organize your collection. Next, find a special place to keep your collection. Places such as a desk drawer, a cabinet, or even under your bed can be good choices. Anyone can have a collection just by showing motivation, imagination, and creativity. Yes, you can do it! So start your collection and have fun!

Page 25 (continued)
1. Krissy, what do you know about coin collecting?
2. Yes, we might start a new collection of oldies music.
3. Collecting things such as buttons, pins, and bottles can be fun.
4. Well, girls might collect dolls, stickers, and stamps.
5. Boys might collect insects, toy trains, cars, and marbles.

Page 26
1. "I remember when we got Rover!" yelled Sally.
2. Sandra asked, "Do you remember how excited we were to take him home?"
3. "He wanted to play all night long," said Kevin.
4. "Rover's favorite thing to do is play with Frisbees," said Sally.
5. Sandra exclaimed, "I like taking him on walks!"
6. "Wow!" said Kevin. "I can't believe we have had Rover for over five years."
7. "Did you do anything special with Rover today?" asked Debbie.
8. Sally answered, "He rode with me to the supermarket."
9. "I took him to the park for a jog," remarked Kevin.
10. "Okay," said Debbie, "he should be ready for a nap!"

Page 27
1. "Eating Healthy"
2. Spider's Design
3. Laughing Elephants
4. The Night Sky
5. Kitty Digest
6. Soccer Buddy, Baseball Billy
7. "The Beautiful Land"
8. Adventures in Racing
9. Allen Morning News
10. Polly, Pioneer Girl

Page 28
1. simile
2. metaphor
3. simile
4. metaphor
5. simile
(Answers for 6-11 may vary.)
6. ice
7. thunder
8. a blanket
9. a melted candy bar
10. a lifetime
11. bright stars
Challenge yourself: Answers will vary.

Page 29
Answers may vary.
1. The brown dog ran quickly to the boy.
2. The sweet young girl played softly with the cuddly kitten.
3. Mother ran quickly to the old rusty mailbox.
4. The shiny new car's horn honked loudly.
5. Father drove the car quickly down the long street.
6. The sweet girl looked happily at her loving parents.
7. They crept quietly into the dark spooky house.
8. The quiet boy and the shy girl sat down carefully.

Page 30
Answers will vary.

Page 31
Answers will vary.

Page 32
A) 3   B) 3
  1   1
  2   2

(Yesterday) I decided to get some fresh air. It had been raining all morning and I was stuck inside with nothing to do. I took my bicycle from the garage. Its sleek colors and racing wheels seemed to be begging for a long ride. (After) I closed the garage door, I climbed aboard and peddled quickly down the street. (Next) I passed my friend's house. I hadn't visited with Billy in a few days, but decided to continue on. (By the time) I stopped at the stoplight to cross the street, I could feel my heart pounding with excitement. I knew the swings would be empty and ready to soar in the air. (Finally) I arrived at the park. To my surprise, Billy was already sitting aboard a swing. He had been waiting for my arrival.

Page 33
Event #1: Planning the boat trip
Event #2: Boating on the lake
Event #3: Getting stuck in the rainstorm
Supporting details will vary.
Challenge yourself: Answers will vary.

Page 34
Answers will vary.

Page 35
Answers will vary.

Page 36
Answers will vary.

Page 37
Answers will vary.

Page 38
Answers will vary.

Page 39
Answers will vary.

Page 40
Answers will vary.

Page 41
1. bizarre, built, realm, remorse, wilt, wither
2. gallon, golden, gorge, utter, wadle, ward
3. freight, fruitful, fudge, fumble, fumigate, function
4. sleazy, sleepily, slicker, slide, slight, slipper

Page 42
1. 262, 260, 259
2. 262, 261, 260
3. 259, 259, 261
4. 260, 260, 262
5. 262, 259, 259
6. 259, 261, 260
7. 260, 262, 262
8. 262, 260, 260
9. 261, 260, 261
10. 261, 259, 259
11. 260, 261, 261
12. 262, 261, 260

Page 43
1. index
2. full title page
3. table of contents
4. glossary
5. copyright information
6. full title page
7. index
8. table of contents
9. table of contents
10. index
11. copyright information
12. index

Page 44
1. Chapter 3
2. 12 pages
3. Answers may vary.
4. Chapter 2
5. 6 chapters
6. Answers may vary.
7. 2 pages
8. Chapter 5
9. Chapter 4
10. Answers may vary.
11. Answers will vary.
12. by chapters

Page 45
1. carpet baggers: 44, hospitals: 53-54, battles: 29-32, 36-42, 50-53, Fort Sumter: 37-38, amputations: 53, Jefferson Davis: 32
2. Gettysburg and Bull Run were battles.
3. They were both generals.
4. pages 23-24
5. amputations
6. before
7. the Blue

Page 48
1. stretched out (Definitions may vary.) Sentences will vary.
2. shot (Definitions may vary.) Sentences will vary.
3. From top to bottom, the numbers read: 3, 2, 1, 5, 4
4. anxious
5. that fireworks just don't appear in the sky
6. "We had waited for this day all year." "It seemed like the day had just started."
7. The parade extended like a snake down several city blocks.
8. Answers may vary. One possible answers is: The fire trucks were as red as cherries.

Page 49
1. a
2. b
3. b
4. d
5. a
6. c
7. c
8. a
9. c
10. a

Page 50

Answers may vary.

"The History of the Fourth of July" | "Let the Fireworks Begin"

- non-fiction
- informative
- includes facts and years

- talks about the Fourth of July
- mentions parades and barbeques

- fiction
- narrative
- includes quotations

Challenge yourself: Answers will vary.

Page 51

Answers may vary.

morning/evening, cold/chilly, morning/evening, beautifully/wonderfully, more rapidly/faster, cancelled/called off, great/super, made/created, hated/liked, inside/outside, warm/hot, remainder/rest, evening/morning, huge/large, shouldn't/should, grumpy/cheerful, unforgettable/memorable

Page 52

1. It's, sale
2. meet, aunt, sea
3. bow, hair
4. beach
5. I'll
6. I've
7. I'll
8. we're
9. she's
10. they've
11. it's
12. don't
13. he'd
14. haven't
15. she'd
16. airport
17. playgroup, airport
18. afternoon
19. upstairs, beanbag
20. supermarket

Page 53

(Anwers for rows 1-6 may vary.)

1. disadvantage, prepay, premix
2. disapprove, unable, unwind
3. misguide, misread, rearrange
4. graceful, swiftly, handful
5. hardly, madly, loveable
6. smoothly, friendly, suspenseful
7. interrogative
8. imperative
9. exclamatory
10. declarative

The corrected paragraph reads:

  Lacey and Jennifer are on the South Lake cross country team. They're dedicated runners who wake every morning at 6:00 a.m. to rush to school to work out with the team. They run three to four miles over a variety of cross country trails. This prepares them for the different courses they might run in a competition. In the fall season, there is a competition each Saturday at Rambler Park in Kingman. Lacey and Jennifer watch what they eat the night before the big race, and they make sure they get a good night's rest. The average trail that the girls will run is two miles. Coach Cleaver is proud of their dedication to the team.

Page 54

1. I enjoy learning more about our nation's leader.
2. George Washington was a wonderful leader.
3. Thomas Jefferson is my favorite president.
4. I wrote a report about President George Bush.
5. We showed illustrations with our report.
6. My mother's parents like to visit us in the summer, and my father's parents like to visit in the winter.
7. I wanted to ask my mother why they didn't visit at the same time, but my brother told me why.
8. My mother's parents live in the southern states, and my father's parents live in the northern states.
9. The president leads our country, and he makes decisions about our nation.
10. When it was first built, the White House didn't have electricity, but it did have an abundance of candlesticks.

Page 55

1. The United States started with thirteen colonies.
2. Massachusetts, Connecticut, Rhode Island, and New Hampshire were the New England colonies.
3. Much of our nation's history took place in Boston, Massachusetts.
4. There was a famous tea party held in the Boston Harbor.
5. The water was swimming with tea.
6. soldiers'
7. nation's
8. flag's
9. horse's
10. men's
11. battleships'
12. dog's
13. fish's
14. The, American Revolution, Britain
15. George Washington, American Revolution
16. Many, Declaration of Independence
17. John Hancock
18. Today, Fourth of July

Page 56

1. Tara and I/We
2. Susan and Toby/They
3. Carter and Tom/They
4. Susan and I/We
5. Tara/She
6. miniature, golf
7. miniature, golf
8. putting
9. bumper
10. small, racing
11. The thrilling ride was finally over after three long minutes.
12. The bright red car went the fastest through the dark tunnel.
13. Cheri drove the bright yellow car to the top of the grassy hill.
14. Mary's small car was not very fast so she took the big blue bus.
15. Phil passed the three cars quickly to finish first in the race.

Page 57

1. Grandpa and Grandma Davis quickly(A) pulled(V) their RV into the driveway.
2. My brother and I excitedly(A) rushed(V) out to meet them.
3. They laughed(V) loudly(A) as they opened the door.
4. My mother ran(V) from inside(A).
5. She had(HV) waited(V) impatiently(A) for their arrival.
6. They were(HV) happily(A) staying(V) with us for two weeks.
7. They usually(A) have(V) gifts for us.
8. I yelled(V) loudly(A) for my father.
9. He was(HV) upstairs(A) shaving(V).
10. He trotted(V) downstairs(A) to greet them.
11. c 12. b 13. c

Page 58

1. C
2. I
3. I
4. C
5. C
6. The Wild Rabbit
7. Tales of My Rabbit
8. "Healthy Living"
9. The Dancing Princess

Answers for 10-14 will vary.

Page 59

1. "When I grow up I want to be an astronaut!" yelled Tim.
2. Craig yelled, "You always change your mind about what you want to be when you grow up."
3. "I just want to be a fireman, astronaut, and policeman," explained Tim.
4. "Maybe you could work for NASA," said Donnie.
5. "Did you know that the stars sometimes form pictures of birds, ducks, and cars?" asked Tim.
6. Red Blvd., Flame Leaf Cr.
7. Oct., Rob Smith Sr.
8. Oak St., Mr. Williams
9. Mon., Nov. 13
10. emphasize, employee, empty, enamel, encounter, encourage
11. chow, chubby, chunk, church, cinema, circle, circuit

Page 60

1. metaphor
2. simile
3. simile
4. metaphor
5. simile

Rewritten paragraphs will vary.